Usborne
1001
Things to spot
at
Christmas
Sticker Book

Alex Frith

Illustrated and designed by Teri Gower

Additional design by Nelupa Hussain

Edited by Anna Milbourne

Contents

Things to spot

Preparing for Christmas is hard work. Join Santa and his team of helpers as they set about making Christmas a magical holiday for everyone. Each scene in this book is full of Christmassy things for you to find and count. There are 1001 things to spot altogether.

Christmas baking

8 cookie cutters

7 gingerbread men

9 sugar mice

8 pastry elves

Each little faded picture shows you what to look for in the big picture.

5 smiling pans   7 white plates   9 festive pies   5 rolling pins   3 pixies with whisks   10 magic cupcakes

15

The number by each faded picture shows how many of that thing you need to find.

When you've found all of each thing, put a matching sticker on top of the faded picture. You'll find the stickers in the middle of the book.

This is Smudge the penguin. He's come to spend the winter with Santa and his hard-working helpers. Can you find him in every scene?

Christmas Land

 **5** elves chopping

 8 reindeer

 4 snow boots

 5 Advent calendars

 **9** Christmas wishes

 **1** Mrs. Claus

 9 festive wreaths

 **10** mail pixies

 **7** elves on sleighs

5

Decorating the tree

6 snowy owls   **7** hot drinks   **10** silver stars   **9** hearts   **3** ladders

6 nutcracker men

7 snowy squirrels

10 pine cones

9 snowdrops

8 snowball pixies

Snowball fight!

5 snowmen

8 dazed pixies

3 snow forts

8 spotted scarves

10 fir trees

8 red elves

10 ice imps

8 yellow elves

3 snow cannons

7 catapults

Santa's workshop

9 dolls

10 teddy bears

8 red levers

7 robot hands

8 toymaker elves

5 oil cans

2 pie elves

10 yellow bows

8 striped balls

6 red cars

11

Winter games

8 flags **6** gnomes **1** musk ox **10** hoops **9** cheering fairies

5 frost monsters

7 racing sleds

9 snowsurfing elves

4 polar bears

9 hockey sticks

Christmas baking

5 smiling pans

8 cookie cutters

7 gingerbread men

9 sugar mice

8 pastry elves

7 white plates

9 festive pies

5 rolling pins

3 pixies with whisks

10 magic cupcakes

Midwinter ball

10 mugs of hot cocoa

6 elves dancing

7 merry mice

8 snow geese

6 pixies skating

7 ice sculptures

9 masks

10 lanterns

7 fiddle players

Use these stickers on pages 4-5.

Use these stickers on pages 6-7.

Use these stickers on pages 8-9.

Use these stickers on pages 10-11.

Use these stickers on pages 12-13.

Use these stickers on pages 14-15.

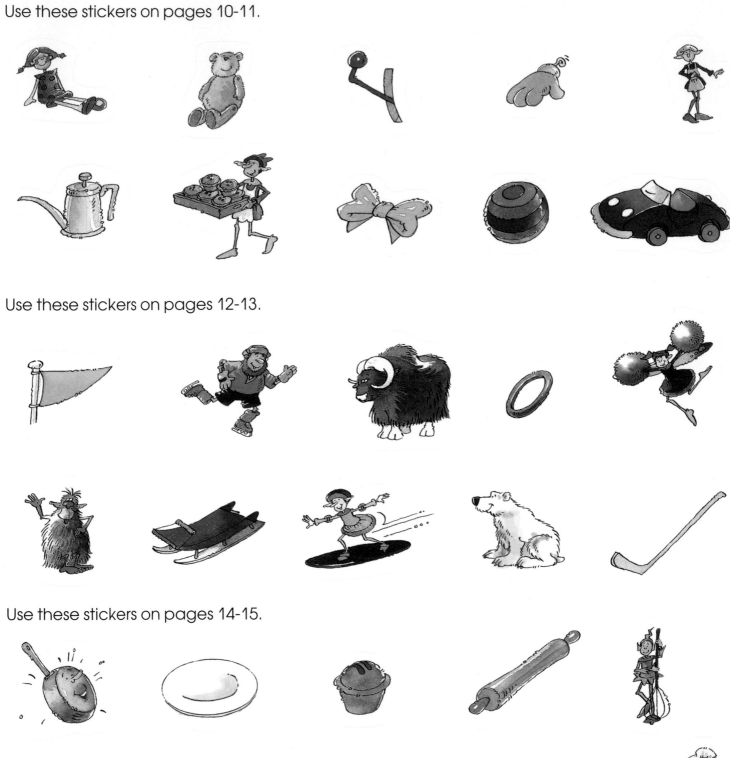

Use these stickers on pages 16-17.

Use these stickers on pages 18-19.

Use these stickers on pages 20-21.

Use these stickers on pages 22-23.

Use these stickers on pages 24-25.

Use these stickers on pages 26-27.

Use these stickers on pages 28-29.

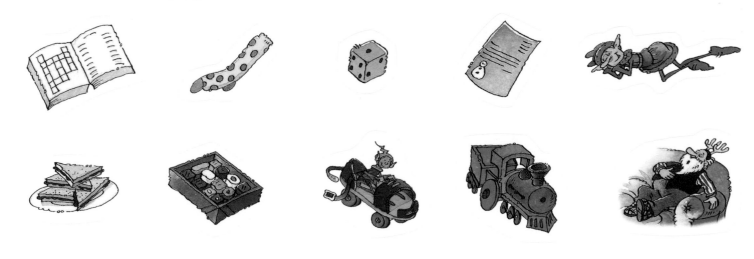

Use these stickers on pages 30-31.

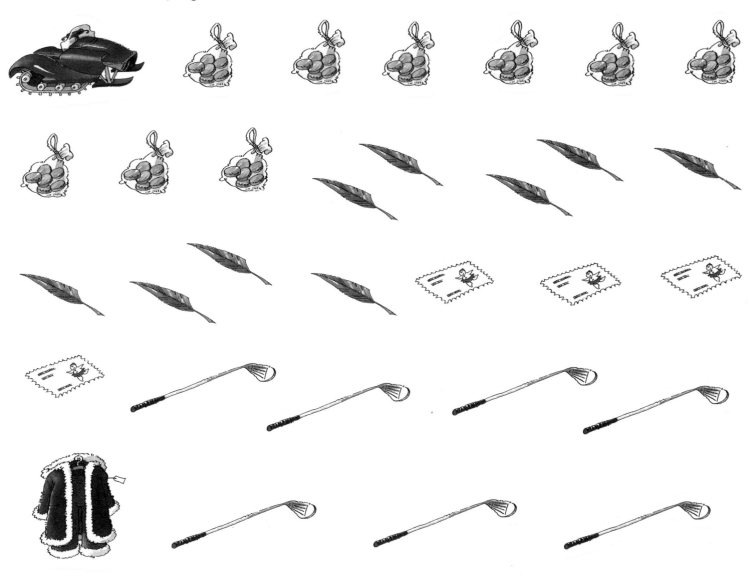

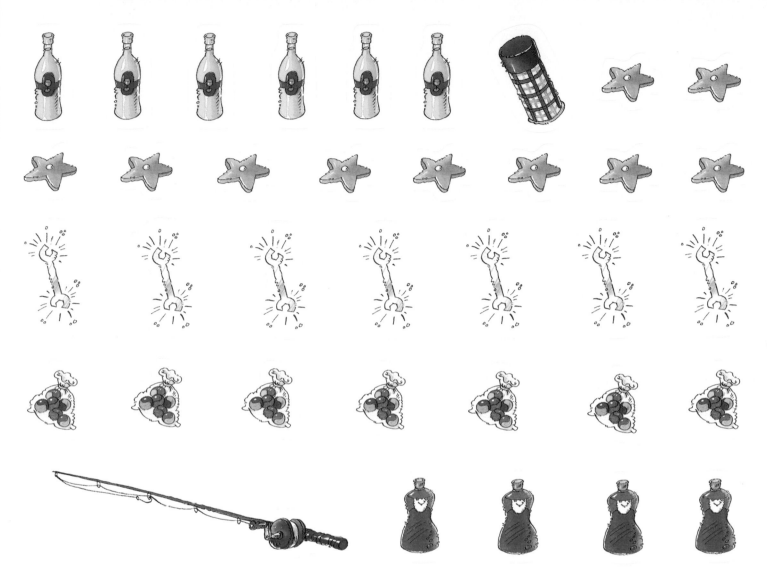

You could reward yourself by sticking one of these stickers on every
page when you've found all the things around the edges.

1 Jack Frost

Reindeer stables

2 fairy supervisors

7 reindeer dinners

6 pixies polishing

8 reindeer brushes

10 bags of magic dust

5 bottles of hoof oil

6 elf mechanics

9 buckets of water

7 paintbrushes

6 baby reindeer

Above the rooftops

4 green
sleighs

6 singing
cats

8 silver
bells

1 town
clock

10 purple
presents

8 streetlights

10 present pixies

9 chimneys

8 strings of lights

7 shooting stars

Down the chimney

8 stockings

4 sleeping cats

3 sprigs of mistletoe

9 scampering mice

8 Christmas angels

9 candy canes

10 building blocks

5 carrots

10 cookies

9 fairy wands

Tropical Christmas

6 sandcastles

10 coconuts

3 boats with lights

2 lighthouses

10 palm trees

9 elves in swimsuits

10 fireworks

5 deck chairs

8 turtles

6 dolphins

Christmas feast

 **10** cranberry pies

 6 yule logs

 7 candles

 10 party hats

 4 Christmas cakes

8 pixies singing

3 gnomes eating pie

10 glasses of fizzy pop

8 sugared apples

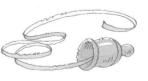

9 party poppers

27

Santa's day off

10 puzzle books

6 socks for Santa

4 dice

10 thank-you letters

9 elves dozing

28

8 plates of sandwiches

7 boxes of chocolates

9 pixies on skates

5 toy trains

1 snoozing Santa

Gifts for Santa

After their Christmas feast, Santa's helpers give him gifts. Look back through the book to find all these gifts, and add a sticker here for each one you find.

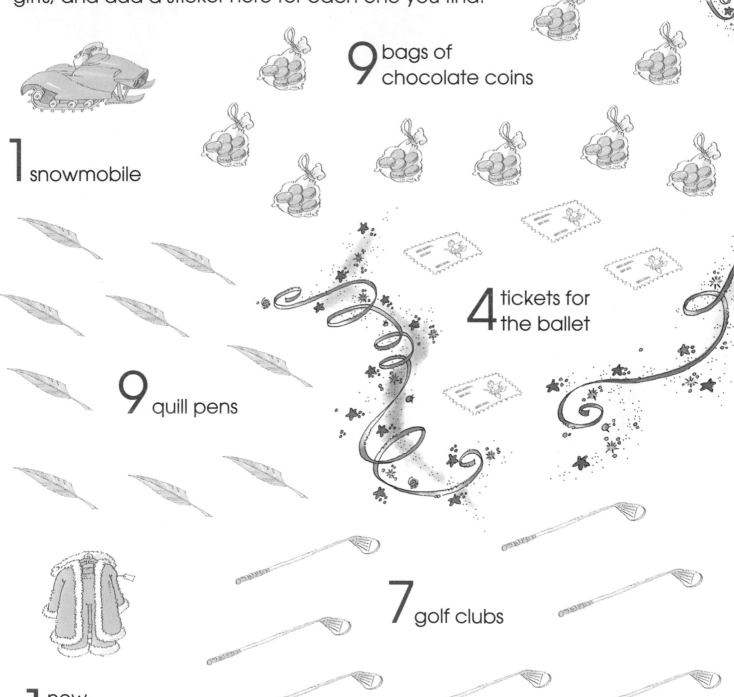

1 snowmobile

9 bags of chocolate coins

9 quill pens

4 tickets for the ballet

7 golf clubs

1 new Santa suit

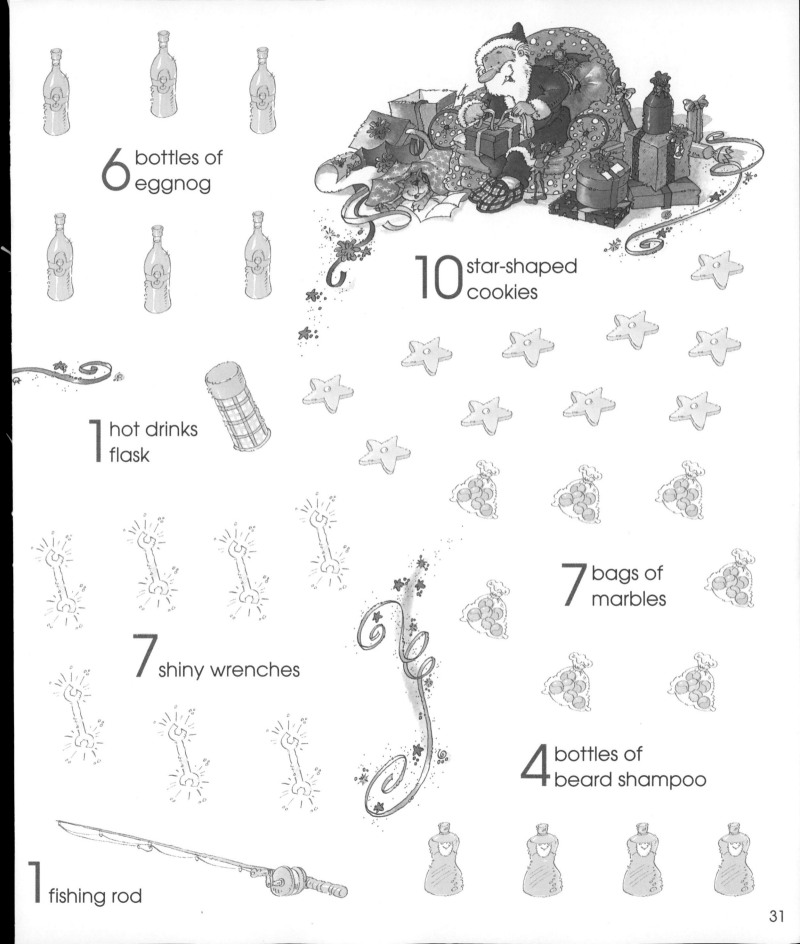

6 bottles of eggnog

10 star-shaped cookies

1 hot drinks flask

7 bags of marbles

7 shiny wrenches

4 bottles of beard shampoo

1 fishing rod

Answers

Did you spot all of Santa's gifts?
Here's where you can find them:

1 snowmobile:
Santa's workshop
(pages 10-11)

4 tickets for the ballet:
Down the chimney
(pages 22-23)

7 shiny wrenches:
Reindeer stables
(pages 18-19)

7 bags of marbles:
Above the rooftops
(pages 20-21)

9 quill pens:
Christmas Land
(pages 4-5)

7 golf clubs:
Snowball fight!
(pages 8-9)

1 fishing rod:
Tropical Christmas
(pages 24-25)

4 bottles of
beard shampoo:
Christmas feast
(pages 26-27)

1 new Santa suit:
Santa's day off
(pages 28-29)

6 bottles of eggnog:
Midwinter ball
(pages 16-17)

10 star-shaped cookies:
Christmas baking
(pages 14-15)

9 bags of chocolate coins:
Decorating the tree
(pages 6-7)

1 hot drinks flask:
Winter games
(pages 12-13)

First published in 2014 by Usborne Publishing Ltd.,
Usborne House, 83-85 Saffron Hill, London EC1N 8RT, England. www.usborne.com
Copyright © 2014, 2009, Usborne Publishing Ltd. The name Usborne and the devices ♀⊕ are Trade Marks of Usborne Publishing Ltd.